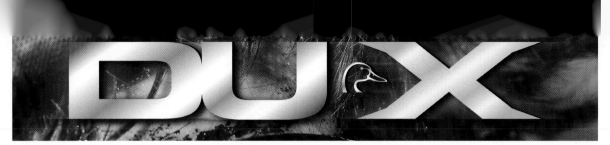

DUX

Runnin' and Gunnin' With Duck Hunting's New Breed

Text by Bill Buckley
Photography by Bill Buckley, David J. Sams, and Lee Thomas Kjos
Foreword by Will Primos

Ducks Unlimited, Inc.
Memphis, Tennessee

Published by Ducks Unlimited, Inc.
D. A. (Don) Young, Executive Vice President, Publisher

Editor: Art DeLaurier
Book Design: Doug Barnes
Cover Design: Lee Thomas Kjos
ISBN: 1-932052-23-2
Published September 2004

Ducks Unlimited, Inc.
Ducks Unlimited conserves, restores, and manages wetlands and associated habitats for North America's waterfowl. These habitats also benefit other wildlife and people. Since its founding in 1937, DU has raised more than $2 billion, which has contributed to the conservation of over 11 million acres of prime wildlife habitat in all fifty states, each of the Canadian provinces, and in key areas of Mexico. In the United States alone, DU has helped to conserve over 2 million acres of waterfowl habitat. Some 900 species of wildlife live and flourish on DU projects, including many threatened and endangered species.

Distributed by The Globe Pequot Press, P.O. Box 480, Guilford, CT 06437-0480.

Library of Congress Cataloging-in-Publication Data

Buckley, Bill, 1958-
   Generation DUX : runnin' and gunnin' with duck hunting's new breed / text by Bill Buckley ; photography by Bill Buckley, David Sams, and Lee Thomas Kjos.
      p. cm.
   ISBN 1-932052-23-2 (alk. paper)
   1. Duck shooting--Pictorial works. 2. Duck shooting--Humor. I. Sams, David J. (David Jazek), 1962- ill. II. Kjos, Lee Thomas, ill. III. Title.
   SK333.D8B8199 2004
   799.2'44--dc22
                      2004018730

Acknowledgments

This book could not have been photographed by three baby-boom-generation photographers had it not been for the generosity and enthusiasm of many young duck hunters who were willing to do pretty much anything we could come up with. While at times you really made us feel like life has passed us by, we're thankful you included us in the fun. Hope we didn't cramp your style too much. There are too many of you to mention here, but we'd like to thank a few people who were truly instrumental to this book.

Bill Buckley would especially like to thank Frankie Ellis and Billy Williams, of Billy Frank's on the River duck-camp fame, and all the good sports who let themselves be photographed there—fellas, you're the best; Jim Kennedy and crew at York Woods for your great hospitality, patience, and accommodation of a strange photographer in your midst; Don Young and sons, big ditto, especially on the patience part; Todd Griffin and friends at Buckshot Lodge for their awesome can-do attitude; ditto for Anthony and Angela Martinez (camo does become you); John Hayes and company, who blow their duck calls like true men; Peyton Randolph for putting up with me (no small feat); Kelly Deiss for risking his life for a good cause; and finally Brian Hauptman, whose love of the goose is legendary.

David Sams would like to thank his beautiful wife, Adrienne, for putting up with his extended hunting trips and long "work" hours; the many folks at DU who helped make this book possible; all the gracious hunters and duck camps that participated, including the world-famous Cross Timbers Hunting Club in Deleon, Texas—thanks Craig, Steve, Sidney; the Broadhurst boys, Trent and Tyler, and all of your college friends who just showed up; Brian Holden and his girls, at Redfish Lodge; Eric Nelson of Port Bay Hunting Club; Tony Hurst of Paradise Hunting Club; Jimmy, at Buckshot Lodge, for cooking such great meals; super models Justin Marks, Scott Isbell, Scott Sommerlatte, Sonny, Jessica James, Ben Hubbard, James Prince, Sawyer Wright, and Paul Brown; Tim Soderquist and the Texas DU college chapters, including David Koch and a dozen other wonderful students who came along for the ride; James and Rick L. Campbell, Chad Starr, Strangler Choke Tubes, Rick's Duck Camp, Ashton Hill Ranch, Larry Gore's Outfitters, Cabela's Ducks Unlimited Catalog, Marshall Outdoor Products, Federal, Winchester, Bismuth, Advantage Wetlands and Max-4 camo, Columbia Sportswear, Beretta USA, Flambeau Decoys, Goose View Industries, Leica Camera Inc., and Rocky Boots.

Lee Kjos would like to thank the Knock 'm Down Boys—Paulie, "Nicky Gangsta," and the "G-Funk Era"—for your all-or-nothin', can-do attitude; Jake, Joe, Bill, A-Rod, and especially Mike, for always—and I mean always—being there; you guys rock. And how thin my life would be without my children—Carmen, Luke, and Gretchen—who provide me with inspiration and keep my spirit and heart a couple decades short of where my wife says they're supposed to be.

Finally, a special thanks to Will Primos and Primos Hunting Calls for their generous support of this project.

Looking at this book brings me back to the days when the guys in the photos could have been me. Duck hunting was an obsession for me in my late teens and early twenties.

At that time, I was working the lunch and dinner shifts at the family restaurant, and hunting on a friend's land near Holly Bluff, Mississippi. I would get up, dress in everything—including my waders—and drive about an hour to Satartia. I would drag my Alligator Boat to a pocket of water in the center of a bean field and try to shoot a limit of ducks by 8:30 so I could be back at work by 10:00 a.m., ready for the lunch-hour rush at the restaurant. Then I would go home for an hour-and-a-half nap before going back to work by 5:00 p.m. I'd work until closing time, around 11:30 p.m., only to get up again at 3:30 a.m. to do it all over again. I was young and obsessed with being there to watch the sun come up on another day in the ducks' world.

At the end of the season, I went back to life without duck hunting . . . but I just didn't feel well. I went to the doctor, who couldn't find anything wrong with me. He sat me down and told me that I needed to quit duck hunting—or hit the lottery and quit working.

Yes, I was obsessed with duck hunting. It was a time that I'll always remember—and cherish. The sight of those ducks cupped up at what seemed to be 400 or 500 yards above my head, coming to that little water hole with wings swooped down at their sides as they fell out of the sky, will always be the highlight of my duck hunting career. It was overwhelming to lie on my back in that Alligator Boat and look straight up, knowing that those ducks were coming in and would be over my decoys within seconds.

I'm sure that whether you're part of the new generation of duck hunters or part of an older one, this book will bring back memories of your love of waterfowl hunting, waterfowl, and the habitats they depend on. It will stand as a tribute to all who carry on the sport's traditions, as well as a reminder that it's our responsibility to share with others our passion for the joys of waterfowling and the obligation to protect the places the birds call home. The bottom line is, you protect what you love.

Will Primos

—Will Primos
Primos Hunting Calls

5

W elcome to Generation DUX: Women love us, ducks fear us, and old guys just can't keep up with us. We're waterfowling's newest breed, runnin' and gunnin' at breakneck speed . . . because we'd much rather crash and burn in a duck marsh than live a dull existence at home on the couch.

Whoever said "youth is wasted on the young" couldn't be talkin' about us. Probably some pot-bellied old couch potato watching *DU TV* and thinking, "Man, I wish I were there."

Dude, we wish you were here, too. But there's a great divide between wishing and doing. Call it the Generation DUX gap. Our best years are ahead of us. And, God willing, so are our best hunts.

With duck season lasting only a couple months, it's full bore ahead. No looking back. No regrets. It's just not our style. Our mission? To go where no duck hunter has gone before. Our motto when we get there? Take no prisoners. Our favorite color wherever we happen to end up? Green . . . as in greenhead.

9

If you're going to run with us there are a few things to get straight right now. First, it's our way or the highway. When it's hunting season, you hunt. And you'd better be on time. Five minutes late? Don't even think about it.

Second, if you don't eat, sleep, and breathe waterfowling, go hunt with guys who consider it only a pastime. You're not going to fit in. Third, if you don't like our driving or how we express ourselves, call 1-555-EAT-DUCK for someone who cares.

Being a Generation DUXer means never having to say you're sorry. We don't question who we are or why we do what we do. All we know is that ducks and geese rule, and pity those who don't feel the same way. Identity crisis? What's that?

Warning, Mom and Dad: This is a goose. These are ducks. These are our sons' brains on geese and ducks.

When waterfowling's in your blood and birds are in the area, you do whatever's necessary to go hunting. And you make sacrifices—like leaving most of your decoys behind in case a Honda Civic pulls over to give you a ride. Hey, it's ducks or bust. Who said it was going to be easy?

Like most duck hunters, DUXers spend much of their time just getting to their blinds. What sets us apart is that we'll do whatever it takes to get there. You know you're washed up when you're not willing to go the extra mile. Not us. Just tell us we can't reach a certain duck hole. Then step aside, girly man, and watch it happen.

But you've gotta have the right attitude. A little sweat never killed anyone, and the farther you have to go, the stronger you get. And the stronger you get, the farther you can go next time. Sure beats pumpin' iron at a gym.

Which is not to say we're gluttons for punishment. Show us a four-wheeler or a duck boat with a mud motor and we're off and runnin'. Give us a boat with some real horsepower and we're movin' fast and furious.

hrow in some heavy metal and serious traction and we're unstoppable. The bigger
the tread, the smaller the sink holes are by comparison. And yes, a tractor pull beats a
ffy pull hands down.

L et's face it: Bigger is always better, and wimpy loads just don't cut it. Neither does running out of ammo midway through the season. But timing is everything, and the cheaper the price, the more we can buy. Boy Scouts we're not, but you can't say we're not prepared for the mother of all migrations.

If you're going to shoot at a duck, you might as well do it right. Nothing says you mean business like a 3½-inch shock-and-awe barrage. Sure, we might get bruised cheeks and shoulders, maybe a detached retina, but there's no getting around it: There is no gain without pain.

act is, moderation just isn't our bag. And if you've got it, why not use it? So what if 99 percent of the time one Mojo will work as well as four and two or three calls are all you need. What about that other 1 percent? Don't worry about looking silly—just never get caught short.

Which is why skimping on decoys is not cool. This dude has the right idea, but he's in serious need of some decoy bags, bungee cords, and a 75-horse outboard. Then he won't have to leave his other eight dozen dekes behind—just one serious wake.

DUXers have left old-fashioned hunters in the dust about three exits back on the telecommunications highway. Like today's military, getting updated information on enemy movement is essential to our success. More important, cell phones and walky-talkies can be a heck of a lot of fun.

Speaking of gadgets and fun, no one told us you can't have fun when the action's slow. The birds have got to fly sometime, and when they do, we'll still be here. Old guys like to say, "He who dies with the most toys wins." We say, "He who lives with the most toys kills more ducks." Dyin's for quitters.

Hi-tech isn't the only way we entertain ourselves in the field. Old-style low-tech games will work in a pinch . . . though you might have to improvise. And when you're really bored, there's nothing like a spitting contest to get the old competitive juices flowing.

Just because something's old doesn't mean we don't use it. A little elbow grease or Aqua-Seal still gets the job done, and nothing works like duct tape. A couple wraps and some spray paint and this Mojo's got its mojo back. Duct tape: Don't leave home without it.

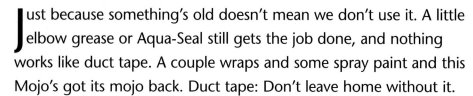

ey, don't hate us for being beautiful.
Whether it's camouflaging up or hors-
ing around, DUXers are all about individual
expression.

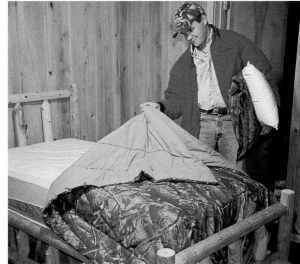

Tricking out duck camp is just another expression of personal taste and individuality. The one and only rule: It's all about the ducks.

Got Beer? We're also all about cramming as much fun into 24 hours as possible. A fire, after all, will last as long as there's fuel to burn. And we'd never dream of crashing until all the beer is gone.

Win, lose, or draw, we'll burn the midnight oil till we've lost all our nickels. To us sleep is just something to do between playing poker and whackin' ducks.

Hangovers? Get outta town! Asleep by 2 a.m., awake at 4...and still feeling like a million bucks. DUXers are like Timex watches: We can take a lickin' and keep on tickin'. Staying sharp is what we do. You know, these waders could be really awesome at our next keg party. Ditto, this trampoline.

Speaking of awesome, imagine having a hottie in camp whose favorite color is camo, who reads DU magazines cover to cover AND who just loves to clean your gun after every hunt. Yeah, right! In your dreams.

But a guy can dream, can't he? When it comes to women, the official DUX philosophy is this: "Shoot for the moon; settle for any skin you can lay your hands on."

Some guys are lucky, though. Play your cards right and you might end up with a wife or girlfriend who really does like putting on camo and who shows you how much she appreciates being taken hunting. Now that's a woman.

For most of us, though, the only tongue we're gettin' has been lapping up swamp water and licking soggy ducks. But action is action. Besides, Labs are DUXers, too. Like us, they appreciate friendly competition, the occasional roll in the hay, and a bellyful of good grub.

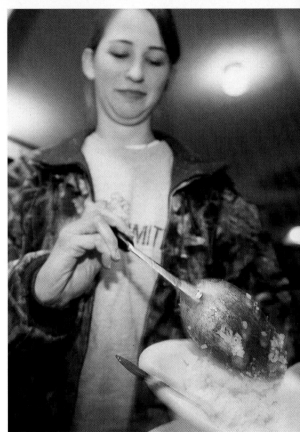

An army may move on its belly, but truth be told, Generation DUX cannot live on duck and beer alone. Chowtime is a highlight at every hunting camp, with a heaping plate rendering the older folks drowsy and heading to bed and the younger set strong and ready for another late night.

Bbut it's breakfast where duck hunters find true sustenance. Salt, fat, nitrates, Mountain Dew: Every essential food group is there, yet not everyone appreciates this fact. No offense, man, but what's that mus you're eating?

How to keep your body going in between meals is where the choices get tough. But a duck hunter on the go can't afford to dilly-dally around. And nobody said it was going to be pretty.

Luckily, with the advent of cell phones, DUXers are not forced to choose between hunting and a hot meal. A lull in the action, a quick trip to the boat ramp, and you can be well fed and back in the blind in no time. *Mmm*, that first slice sure tastes good . . .

The last slice isn't too bad, either, you can pry it away from Fido. When it comes to dogs and food, we tend to be philosophical: A dog's gotta eat, too, and as long as there's something left for us, no harm done.

When you think about it, dogs bust their tails even more than we do. It's only right that we give 'em the occasional boost, even if getting wet defeats part of the reason for having a retriever.

It's not like duck hunters aren't used to getting wet. When you fly too close to a flame you're going to get burned. When you're a waterfowler...well, you know. Fact is, water is part of our everyday world; we revel in it.

Ditto for mud. If a duck hunter were afraid of a little mud, he'd never get anywhere. He'd spend half the season crying into his Bud Light. Where the rubber no longer meets the road—that's where we want to be. And if we get stuck? Get out and start pushin', 'cause we're not gonna get any ducks here.

Cut our losses and turn back? What's the matter, old man, afraid of a little mud? When Generation DUX is on a mission, there's no turning back. There's no playin' it safe. Being a weenie gets you nowhere. Now punch tha gas pedal and go!

O f course, even we have our limits. But if you're gonna get wet and muddy, at least do it right. And have a sense of humor about it. Just like with mallards, let the water roll right off your back.

Who said you can't get points for style. On an Olympic diving scale—a 3.5 with that splashy water entry. Then again…wait…the boat is still afloat! The decoy spread still arranged flawlessly! These guys aren't bad at all. Total score: 8.5.

Oooooh that water's got to be cold! Drain out what you can, though, and you're ready to start hunting again. The stones? Well, they'll be back, too...eventually.

When you cast your decoys into uncharted waters, you accept certain risks. In which case DUXers suck it up and take it like real men.

*S*ome risks, however, can catch even us off guard. Who's the girly-man now, big boy?

Still, never accuse a DUXer of not having the will to take those last few steps, those precious ten yards, that so often separate failure from success. We will not be denied.

What matters most is that we're there, locked and loaded, when the flight begins. And when we put that call up to our mouths and hammer out the first greeting call, everything bad that happened up to that point suddenly doesn't matter. Because calling is ultimately why we hunt.

Calling is how Generation DUX best expresses itself. Sure, we like to hear ourselves talk, but we also want others to listen. Sometimes older folks just don't understand us. Ducks and geese almost always do. Wanna really be heard? Try jammin' with a bunch of your buddies.

It's the ultimate male bonding, the best way to make a rainy-morning hunt last before heading back to civilization. Duck calls fulfill every guy's dream of being a rock star and give new meaning to the expression, "Man, that really blows!"

Ducks calls have other applications, too. Wanna let the old man know he screwed up by not going hunting? Wanna give phone solicitors a blast of Miss Suzie when they ask for the lady of the house? Go ahead...make our day.

S ad to say, but although calls can handle the most insidious solic itors, even electronic calls cannot overcome most snow geese. When the going gets tough, DUXers are forced to get down and dirty. This cow ain't takin' no for an answer.

And this is one woman you better hold on to. Mom will not be amused if you let your sister fall in the mud . . . but Dad might get a chuckle out of it.

It's one thing to take a picture of your girlfriend along for the ride; quite another to watch her pull the trigger. (In case you're wondering, it's true: Now that she's a blond, she's definitely having more fun.)

Isn't this even better than watching female mud wrestling on cable? You betcha, dude!

Nothing's sexier to a DUXer than a girl in camo who's not afraid to get down and dirty. But be careful what you wish for: Choose wisely, or having a hunting girlfriend may not be worth the effort.

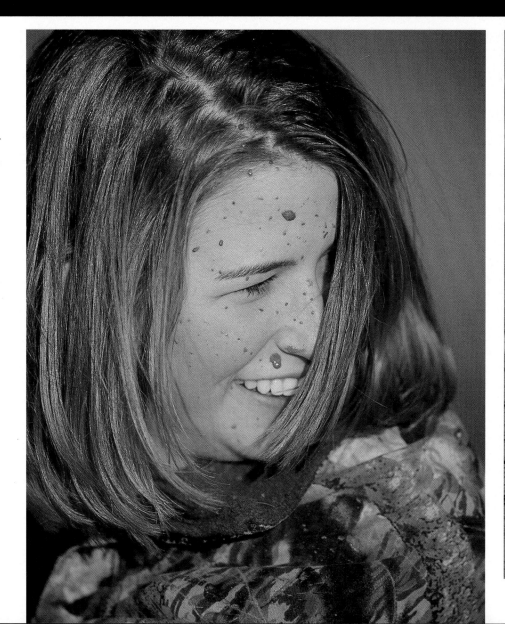

Let's face it, DUXers work hard enough a it is. And we've got to conserve our energy.

Down time? It's catch as catch can in DUX land. A nod here, a wink there . . .

. . . And before you know it, we're up and at it again—stronger, faster, better than the day before.